THE BIG ZODIAC COLORING BOOK

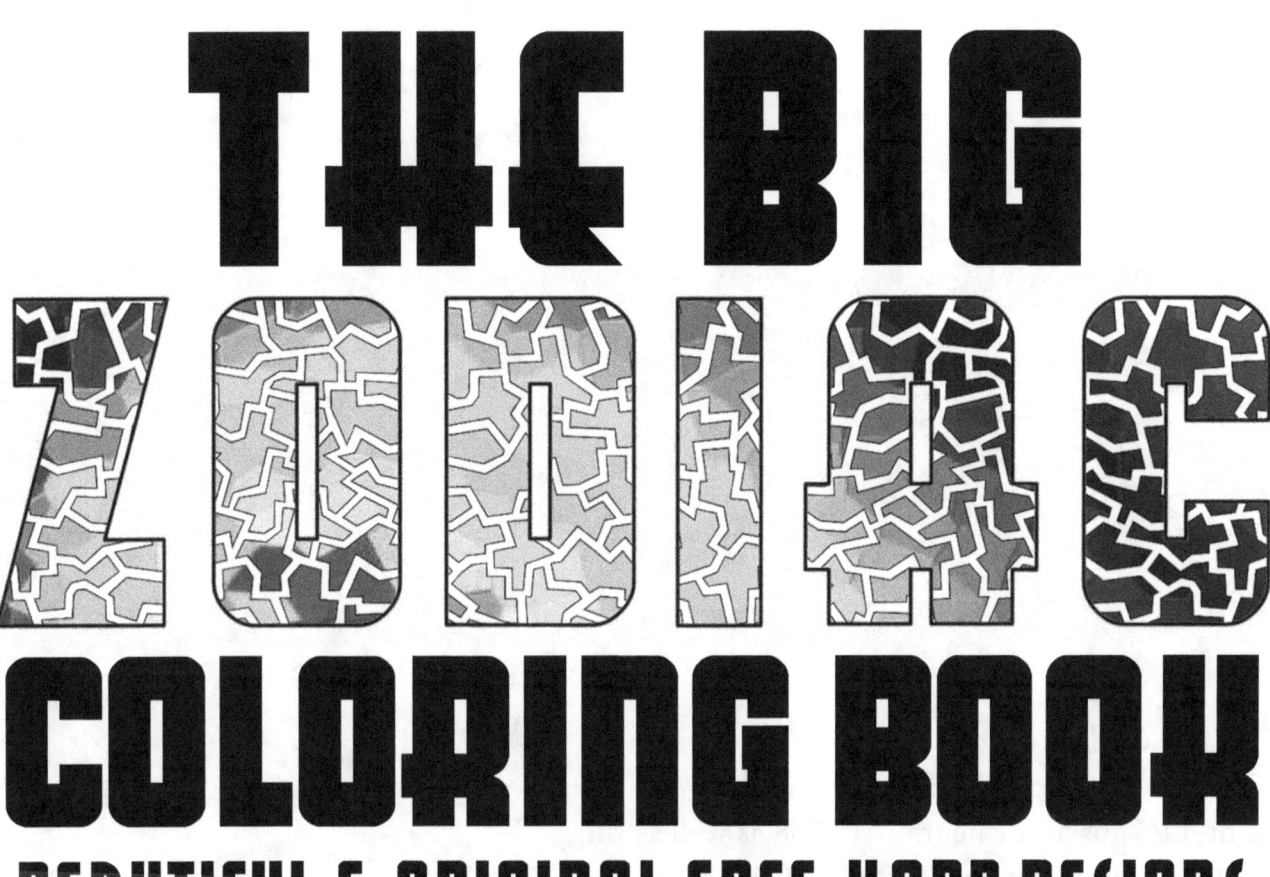

BEAUTIFUL & ORIGINAL FREE-HAND DESIGNS FOR YOUR COLORING ADVENTURE

NOT YOUR AVERAGE COLORING BOOK!

BY CHRIS CHONG

INTRODUCTION

Firstly, a big **Thank You** for purchasing **The Big Zodiac Coloring Book.**

As stated, this is **Not Your Average Coloring Book!** The designs in this book are creations that will challenge the mind as you will first have to find the images blended within.

The idea behind the designs were conceptualized way back in the 1990's inspired by jigsaw puzzles and batik prints. It was while on a two hour flight having flipped through the inflight magazine and with nothing else to do, the prints on the aircrafts seat covers planted the seed for the creation.

I hope you will find your coloring journey with this book not only enjoyable but an adventure into your own imagination and creativity.

Do Not Limit Yourself… Let Your Imagination Flow!

Thank You once again

Chris Chong

… and please do visit **purplefishdigitalmedia.com** for more of my designs.

Before you embark into your coloring journey, below are some pointers to prevent smudging the pages should you happen to use inks that may bleed through the other side of the paper.

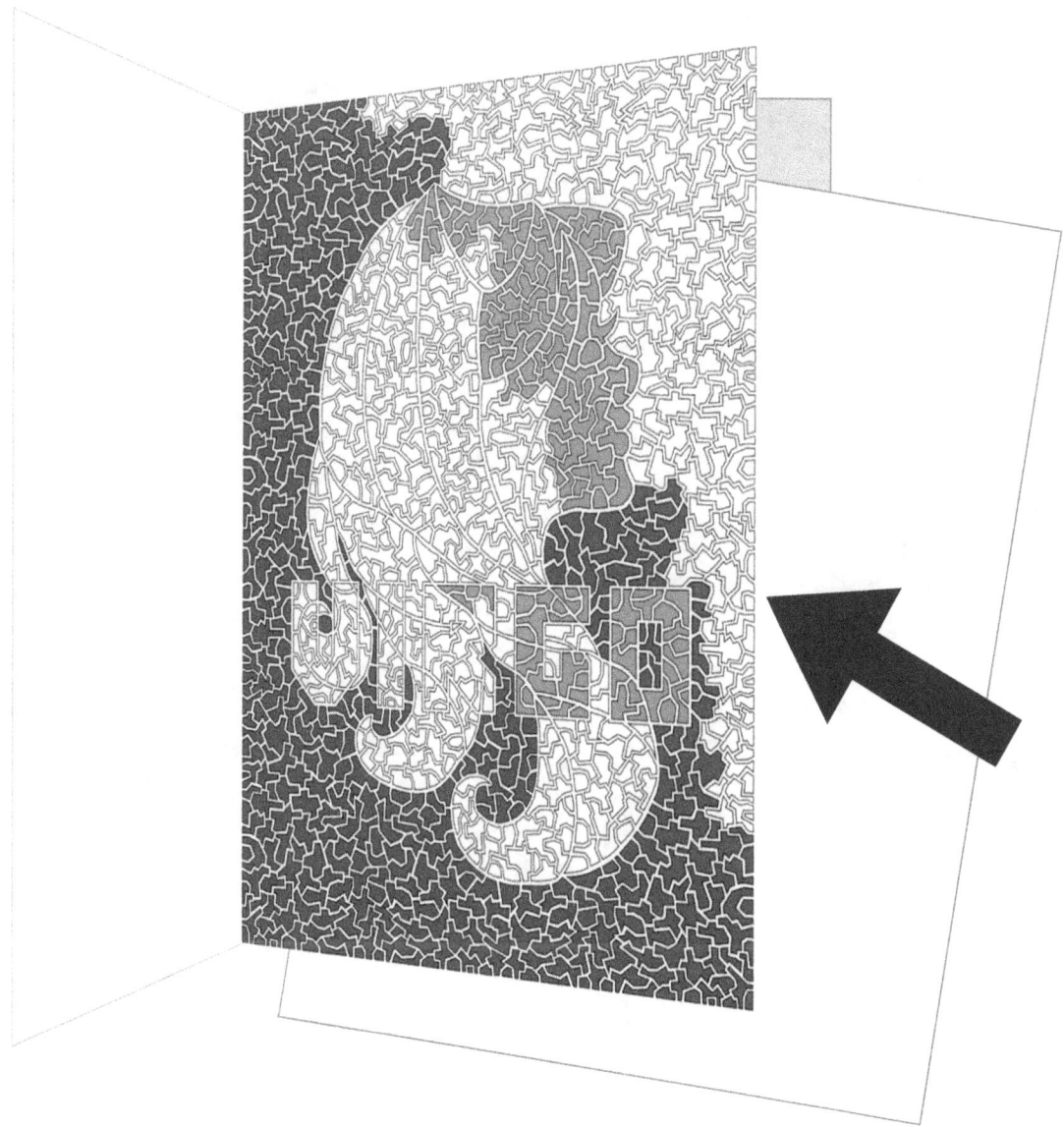

To prevent colors bleeding through, you may want to insert a piece of thick paper in between the doodle and the next page as shown above.

I hope you enjoy this book and Happy Coloring!

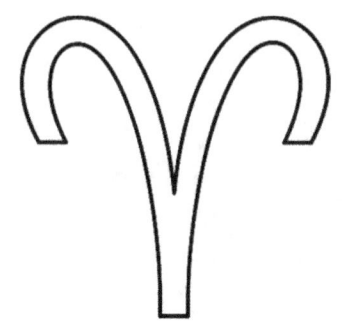

ARIES

March 21 - April 19

Confident, Courageous, Determined, Enthusiastic, Honest, Optimistic, Passionate

Aries is the first sign of the zodiac, and as leaders of the pack, you can certainly be sure they are the first in line to get things going.

As a fire sign, like Leo and Sagittarius, it is in their nature to take action, and sometimes rushing into it too brashly without thinking about it well first.

Among the great strengths of the Aries-born are perhaps their initiative, courage and determination. They just love to get things going, taking that journey fearlessly with their spirit of competitiveness and dynamism.

Can You Find The Images?

If you are having a challenge finding them, just flip to the back of the book for some coloring guides. Remember... Do Not Limit Yourself... Let Your Imagination Flow!

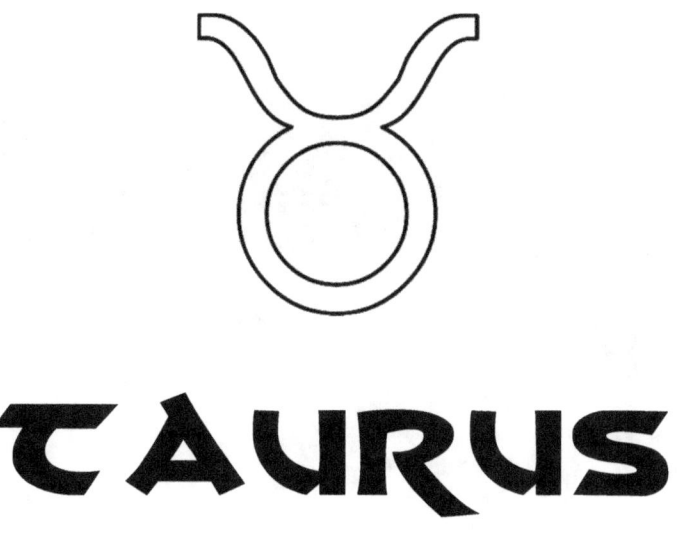

TAURUS

April 20 - May 20

Ambitious, Devoted, Patient, Practical, Reliable, Responsible, Stable

Taurus is the second sign of the zodiac. Those born under this sign love the rewards of the game unlike the Aries-born, who loves the game, and you can be sure they will go all out to get them.

Taurus is an earth sign and they have been known for being overprotective of their loved ones. They are really good at sticking to their projects until successfully completed and are great in making money too.

Dogged determination, loyalty and stability are just some of the great strengths of the Taurus-born. These bulls just want to get the job done, and get it done well they certainly will ultimately achieving the rewards they so fervently crave.

Can You Find The Images?

If you are having a challenge finding them, just flip to the back of the book for some coloring guides. Remember... Do Not Limit Yourself... Let Your Imagination Flow!

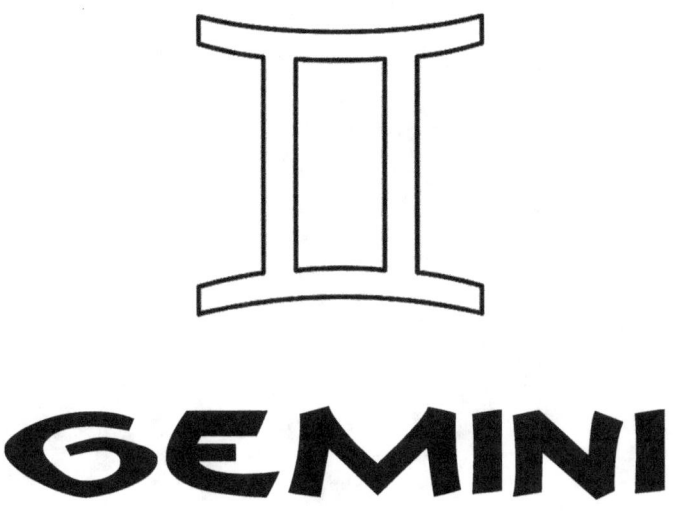

GEMINI

May 21 - June 20

Adaptable, Affectionate, Curious, Expressive, Gentle, Quick-Witted, Sociable

Gemini is the third sign of the zodiac and those born under this sign are never lack of any conversation as they simply love to talk.

Gemini is an air sign and is ruled by Mercury, the planet that represents writing, communication and teaching others thus the Gemini-born is concerned with almost all aspects of the mind.

Effective communication skills and the ability to think clearly are some of the well known strengths of those born under this zodiac sign and they certainly make charming companions as they love to share themselves with their friends.

Can You Find The Images?

If you are having a challenge finding them, just flip to the back of the book for some coloring guides. Remember… Do Not Limit Yourself… Let Your Imagination Flow!

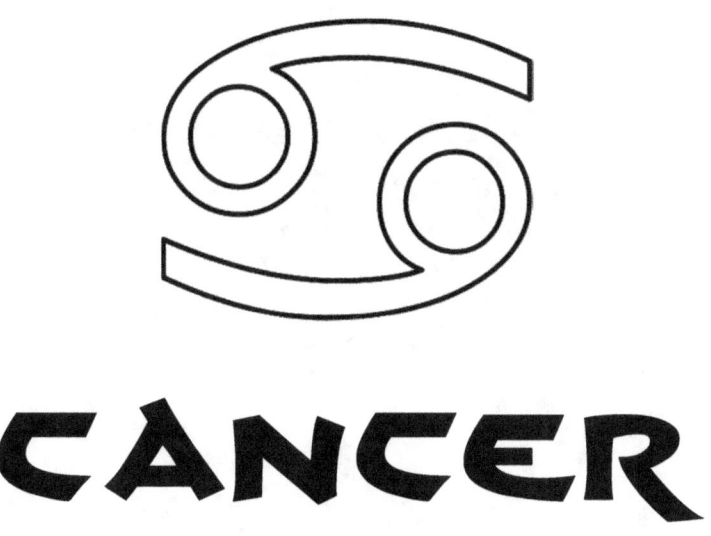

CANCER

June 21 - July 22

Generous, Emotional, Imaginative, Loyal, Persuasive, Sympathetic, Tenacious

Cancer is the fourth sign of the zodiac cycle and those born under this sign take great pleasure in the comforts of family and home.

Cancer is ruled by the Moon and as with the moon's many phases of the lunar cycle, those born under this zodiac sign have been known to experience fleeting emotional patterns with their own internal mysteries that they are unable to control.

The tenacity with which these people protect their loved ones is certainly one of their greatest strengths. A sense of peace and a comfortable home are pretty much what keeps the Cancer-born happy.

Can You Find The Images?

If you are having a challenge finding them, just flip to the back of the book for some coloring guides. Remember… Do Not Limit Yourself… Let Your Imagination Flow!

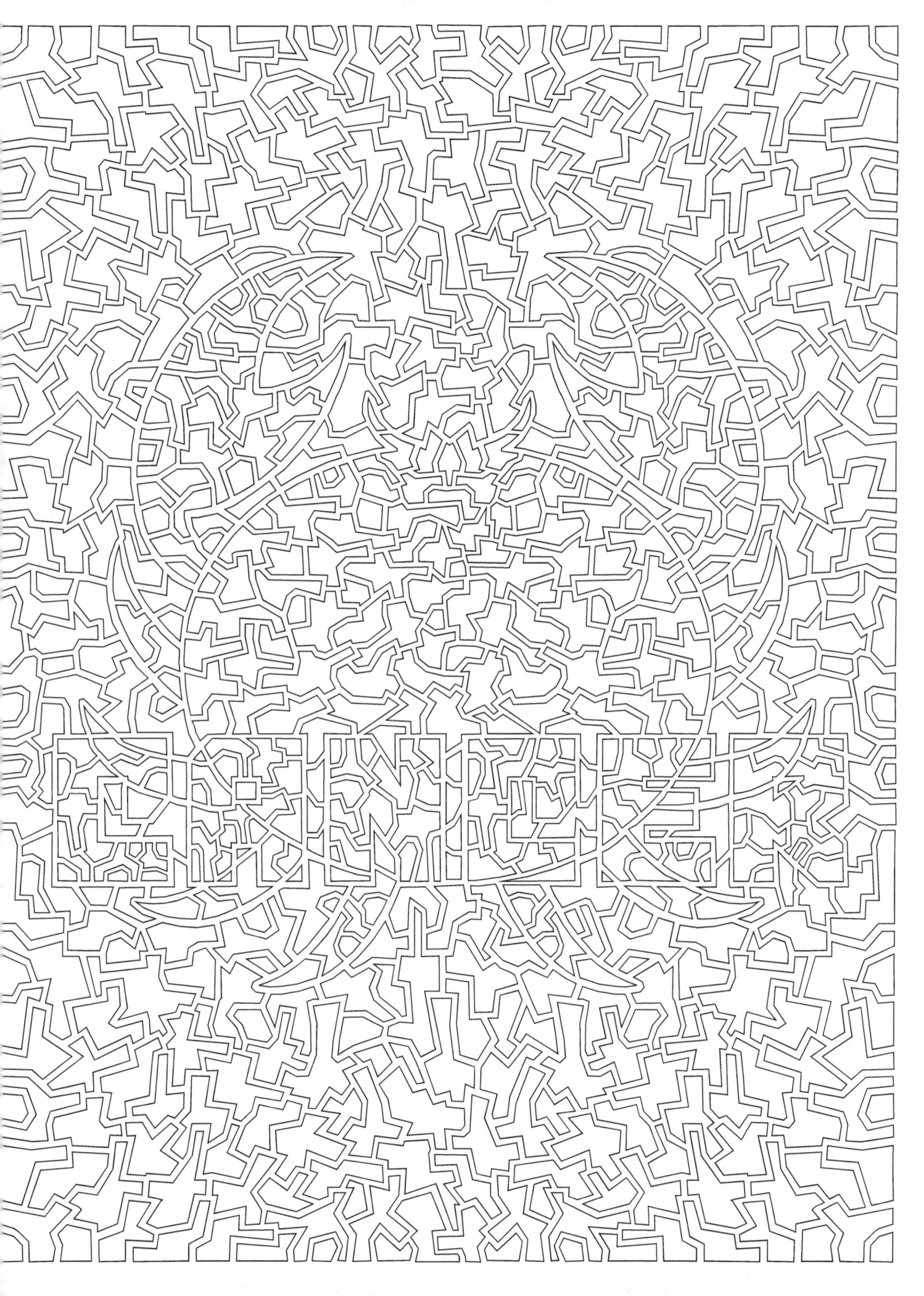

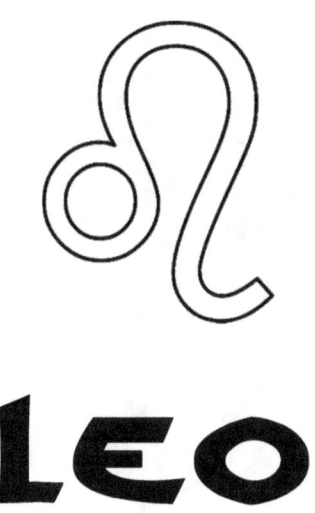

Leo

July 23 - August 22

Cheerful, Creative, Generous, Energetic, Humorous, Passionate, Warm-Hearted

Leo is the fifth sign of the zodiac and those born under this zodiac sign do certainly stand out as they love being on the center stage. They will always expect to have a good time and just love life itself.

Leo is a fire sign, like Aries and Sagittarius, and the Leo-born have the great ability to solve even the most difficult problems using their minds. They will also take the initiative to tackle various complicated situations that may come along their way.

Creativity, leadership and idealism are some of the greatest strength for the Leo-born. These lions are also ambitious so they are likely to accomplish a lot in their lifetime and will have fun while they are doing so too.

Can You Find The Images?

If you are having a challenge finding them, just flip to the back of the book for some coloring guides. Remember… Do Not Limit Yourself… Let Your Imagination Flow!

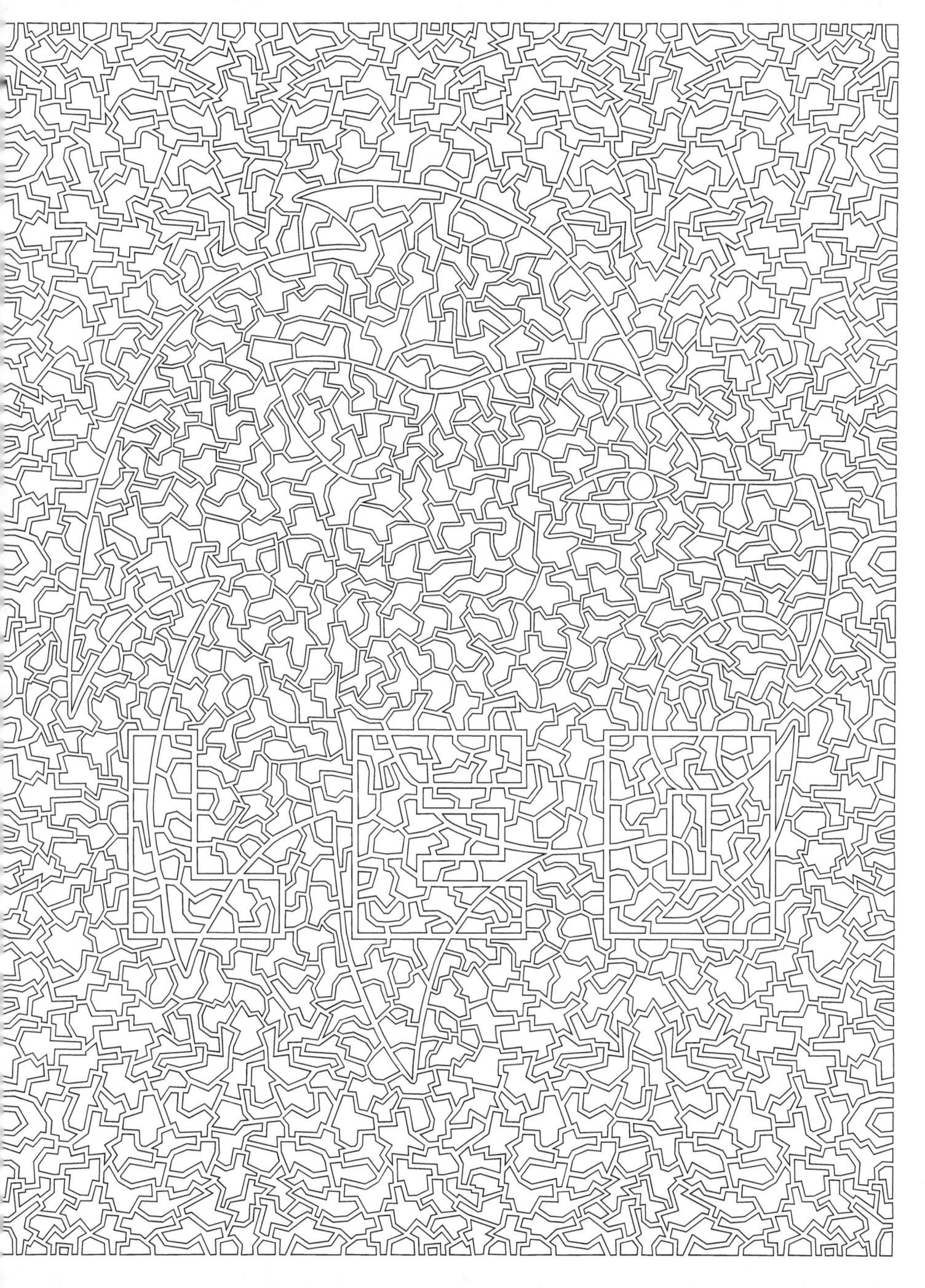

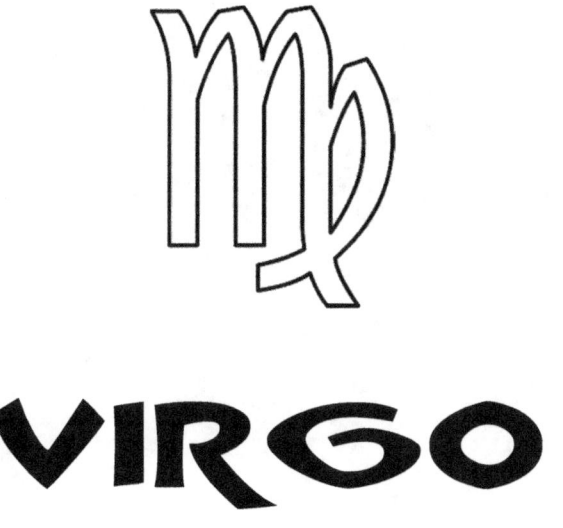

VIRGO

August 23 - September 22

Analytical, Hardworking, Intelligent, Kind, Loyal, Practical, Reliable

Virgo is the sixth sign of the zodiac cycle those born under this sign are conservative and like to have things well organized in their lives.

As an earth sign, the Virgo-born tend to have very organized lives and even if they appear to be messy, you can be sure they have well defined points strictly in their minds for their goals and dreams.

Attention to detail, practicality and a sharp mind are some of the Virgo-born's great strengths making them essential helpmates when their willingness to serve are merged.

Can You Find The Images?

If you are having a challenge finding them, just flip to the back of the book for some coloring guides. Remember... Do Not Limit Yourself... Let Your Imagination Flow!

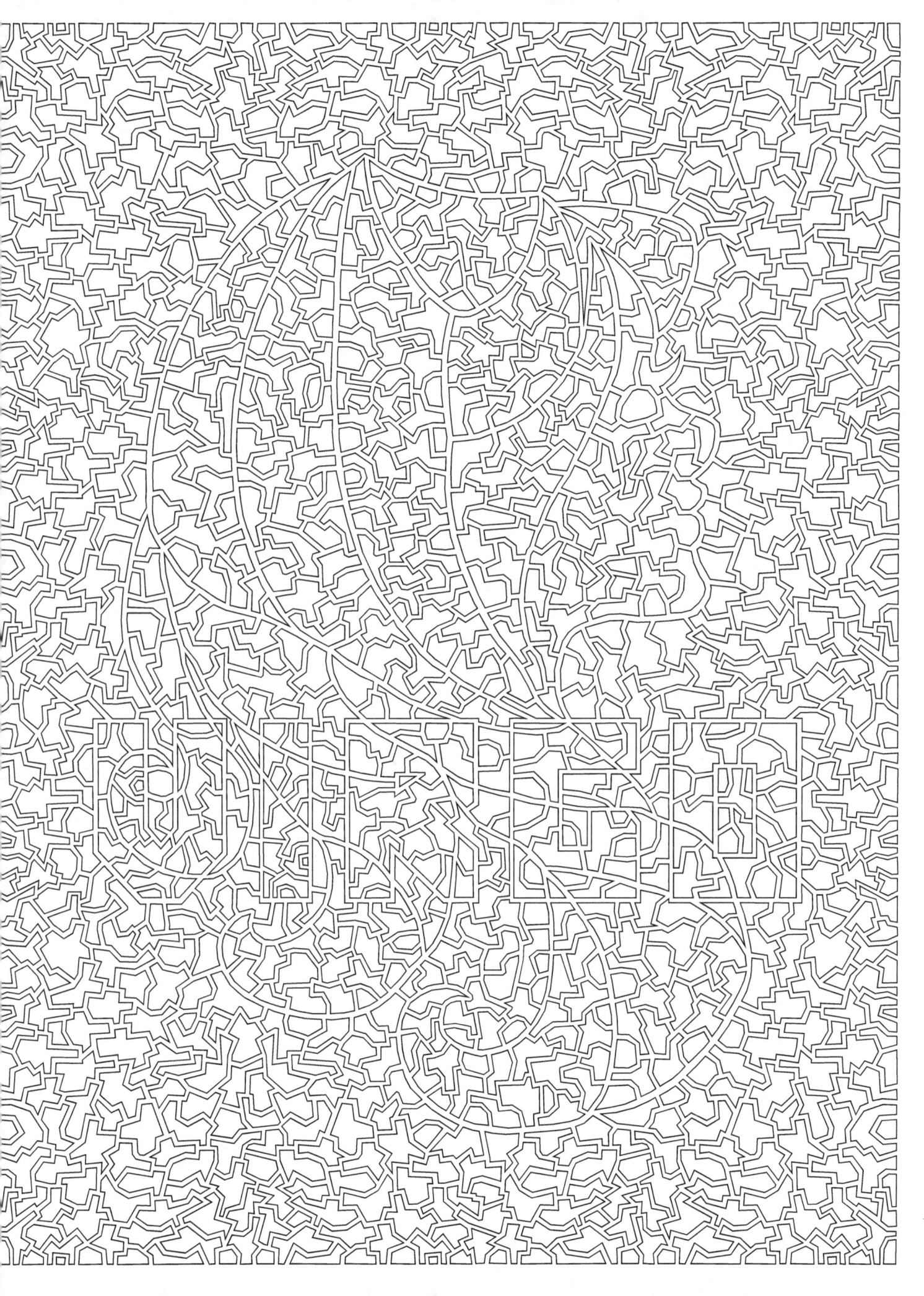

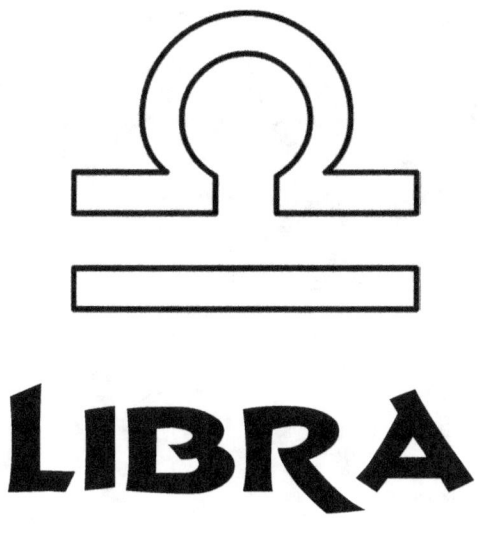

LIBRA

September 23 - October 22

Balanced, Cooperative, Diplomatic, Gracious, Just, Social, Tactful

Libra is the seventh sign of the zodiac and focusing and relating to others are what's first and foremost for those born under this zodiac sign.

Venus, who is a lover of beautiful things, is the planet that rules Libra, so it is the quality and not quantity that is always placed more important for those born under this sign.

Their quest for peace, harmony and fairness are some of the greatest strengths of the Libra-born. They are also known as the great diplomats of the zodiac, like the symbol of the Scales that this zodiac is associated with.

Can You Find The Images?

If you are having a challenge finding them, just flip to the back of the book for some coloring guides. Remember... Do Not Limit Yourself... Let Your Imagination Flow!

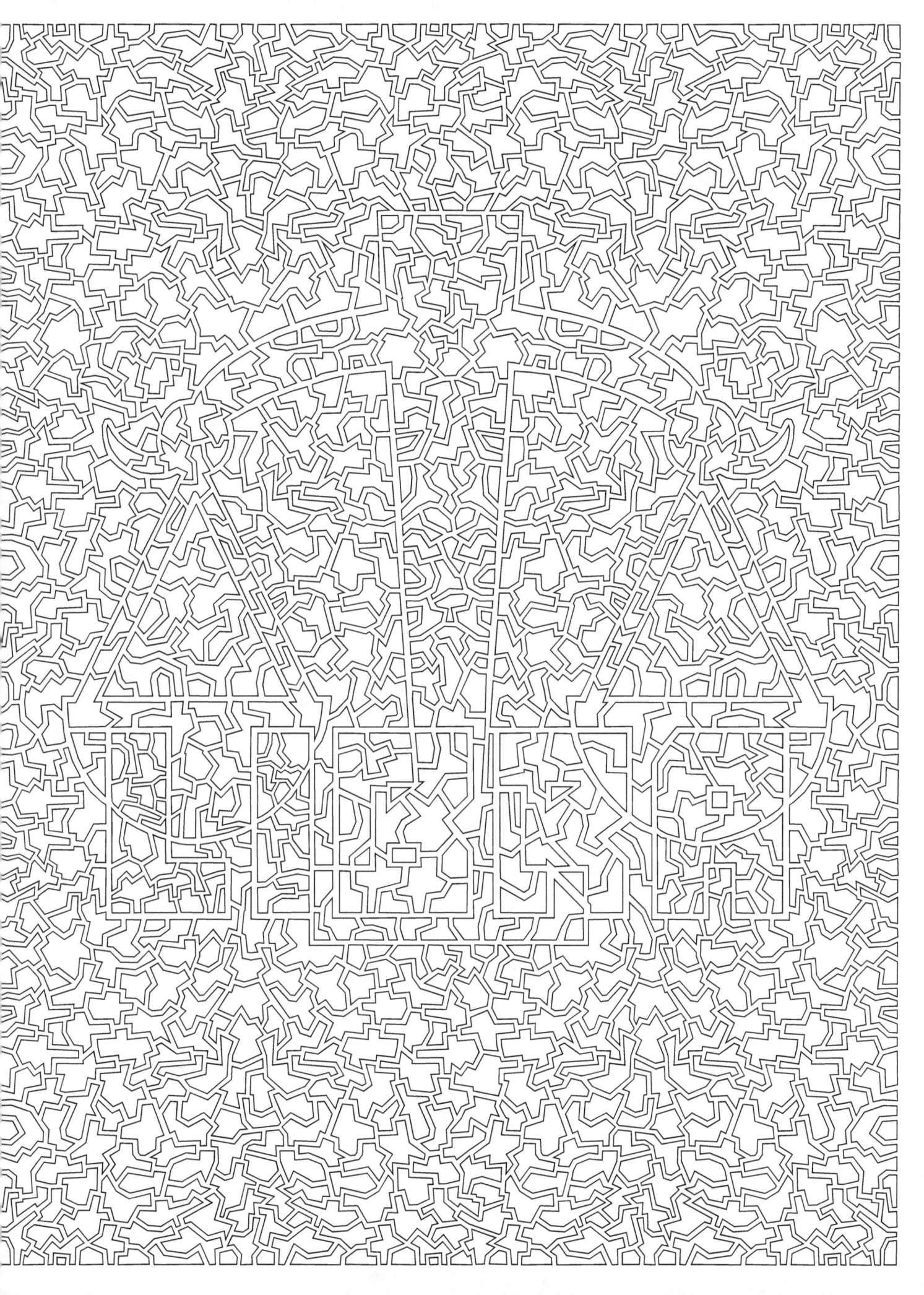

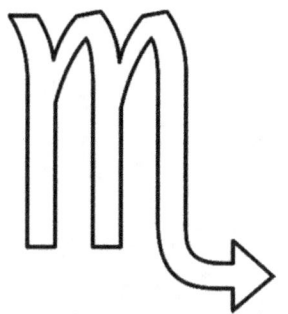

SCORPIO

October 23 - November 21

Brave, Dynamic, Loyal, Observant, Passionate, Resourceful, Stubborn

Scorpio is the eighth sign of the zodiac and learning about others is perhaps the Scorpio-born's ultimate mission and they are dead serious about it.

The ruler of Scorpio is Pluto, the planet of regeneration and transformation. Cool, calm behavior and a mysterious appearance are some characteristics known for those born under this zodiac sign.

With passion, motivation and determination, these Scorpio-born do not know the word 'quit' and you can be sure they will usually get the job done.

Can You Find The Images?

If you are having a challenge finding them, just flip to the back of the book for some coloring guides. Remember… Do Not Limit Yourself… Let Your Imagination Flow!

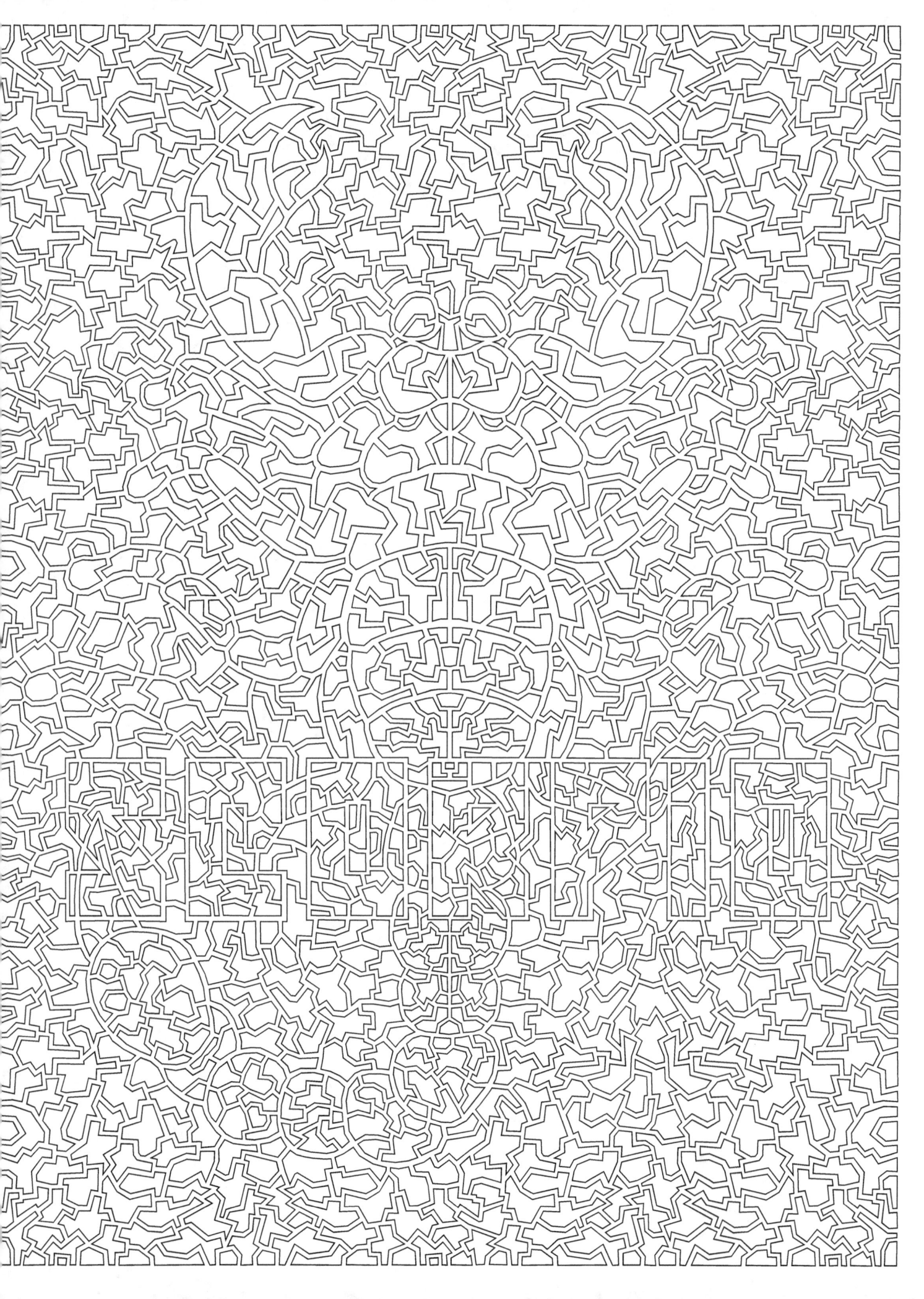

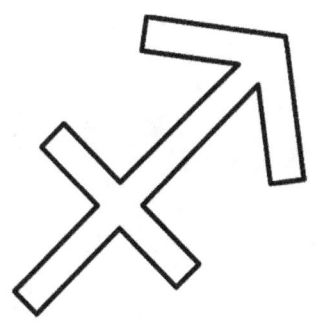

SAGITTARIUS

November 22 - December 21

Adventurous, Enthusiastic, Generous, Idealistic, Intellectual, Philosophical, Positive

Sagittarius, the ninth sign of the zodiac, are truth-seekers. Talking to others and hitting the road are what the Sagittarius-born will do to get some answers.

Jupiter, the largest planet of the zodiac, is the ruler of Sagittarius. With unbounded enthusiasm, those born under this zodiac sign possess an intense curiosity as well as a great sense of humor.

The philosophical, wide-open and curious nature are some of the strengths of the Sagittarius-born. Knowledge and truth are what they seek together with their eagerness to share their explorations with others.

Can You Find The Images?

If you are having a challenge finding them, just flip to the back of the book for some coloring guides. Remember... Do Not Limit Yourself... Let Your Imagination Flow!

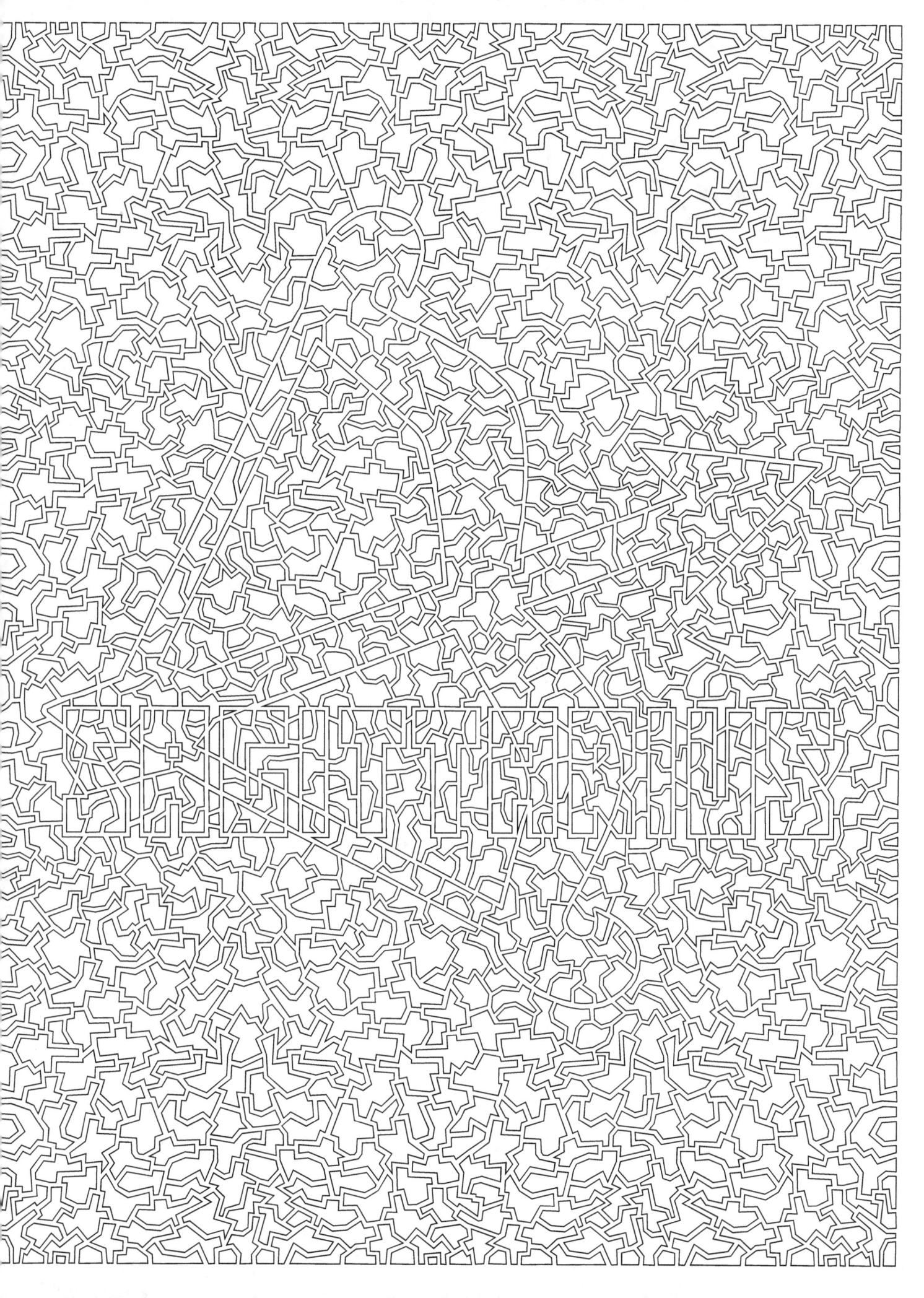

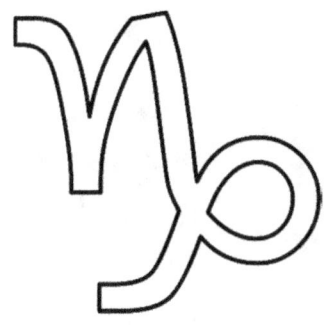

CAPRICORN

December 22 - January 19

Ambitious, Conservative, Determined, Disciplined, Helpful, Practical, Responsible

Capricorn, the tenth sign of the zodiac, those born under this sign are considered to be the hardest working of the lot. You can find them in the office happily putting in a full day's work as they realize that it is most likely what it takes to get them to the top.

Capricorn is an earth sign and for those born under this sign, there is nothing more important in life than family. They are also masters of self-control and have the potential to become great managers and leaders in the business circle.

The determination to succeed with the willingness to work hard alongside their unbounded discipline are some of the greatest strengths of the Capricorn-born.

Can You Find The Images?

If you are having a challenge finding them, just flip to the back of the book for some coloring guides. Remember... Do Not Limit Yourself... Let Your Imagination Flow!

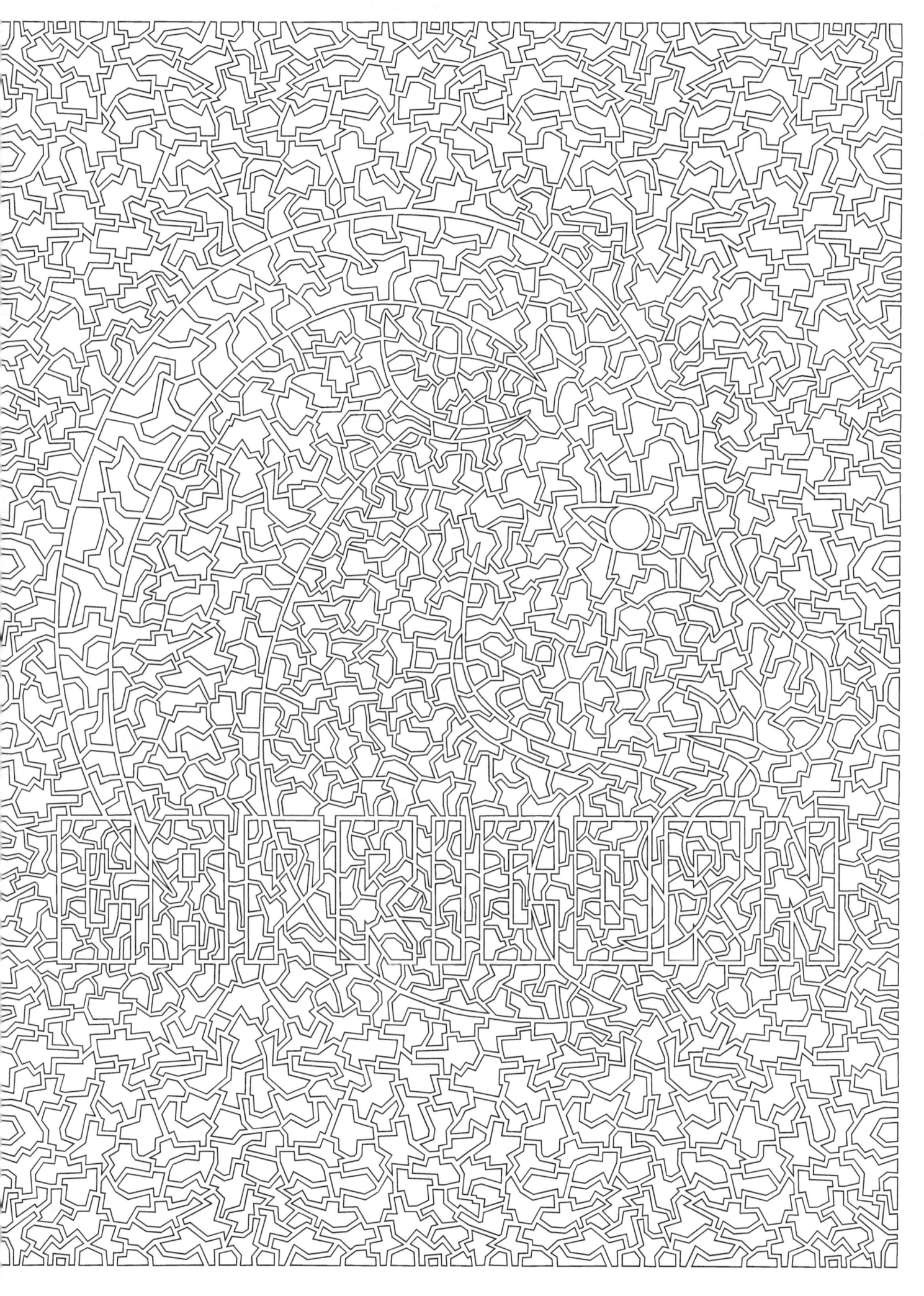

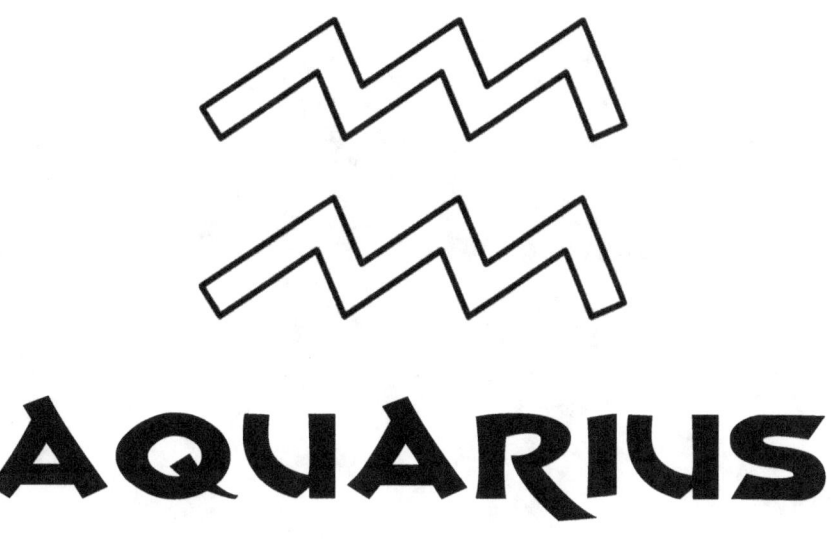

AQUARIUS

January 20 - February 18

Affectionate, Creative, Curious. Friendly, Independent, Original, Progressive

Aquarius is the eleventh sign of the zodiac and those born under this sign are the humanitarians, philanthropists who are keenly interested in making the world a better place for everyone.

As an air sign, the Aquarius-born will use their minds at every opportunity that presents itself. Having no mental stimulation will cause them to be easily bored and lack the motivation to achieve their best results in their endeavors.

Their humanity, intellect and vision with the determination to help everyone they can along the way to make the world a better place are the great strengths of the Aquarius-born.

Can You Find The Images?

If you are having a challenge finding them, just flip to the back of the book for some coloring guides. Remember… Do Not Limit Yourself… Let Your Imagination Flow!

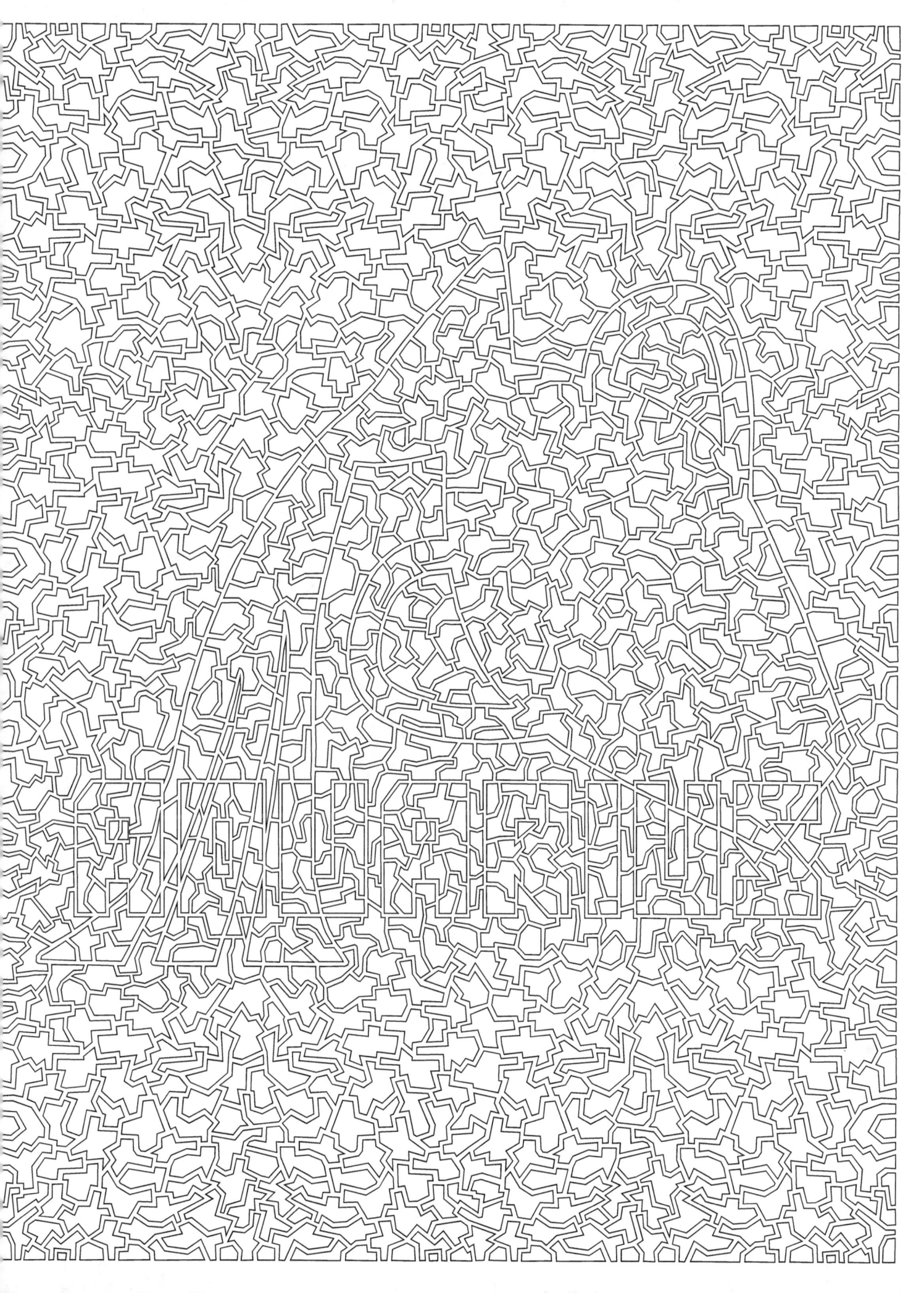

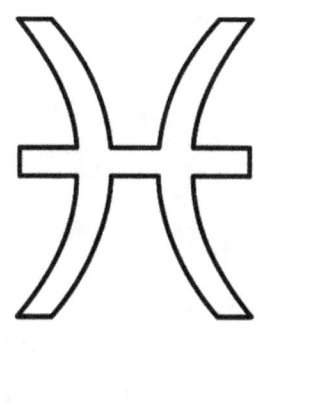

PISCES

February 19 - March 20

Artistic, Caring, Compassionate, Generous, Faithful, Intuitive, Wise

Pisces is the twelfth and final sign of the zodiac cycle and with it those born under this sign incorporates many of the characteristics shown by the previous eleven.

Neptune, which is connected to music, is the ruling planet and the musical preferences for the Pisces-born will become apparent in the early stages of their lives. They also have great artistic talents and are known to be the most intuitive compared to the others.

Some of the great strengths of the Pisces-born are their compassionate and charitable nature. As such they love to help others and will do so in some of the most imaginative ways possible.

Can You Find The Images?

If you are having a challenge finding them, just flip to the back of the book for some coloring guides. Remember... Do Not Limit Yourself... Let Your Imagination Flow!

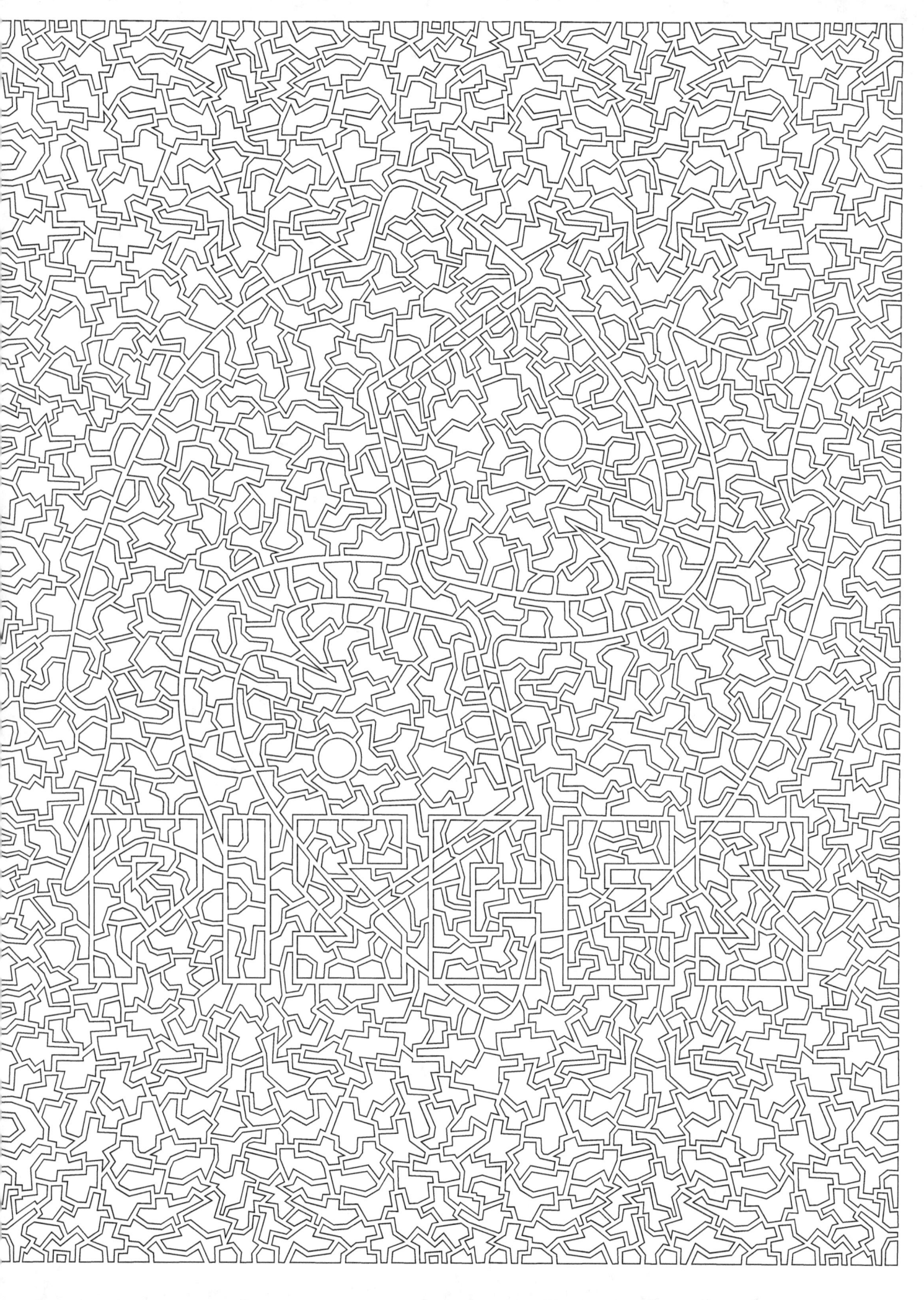

COLORING GUIDES

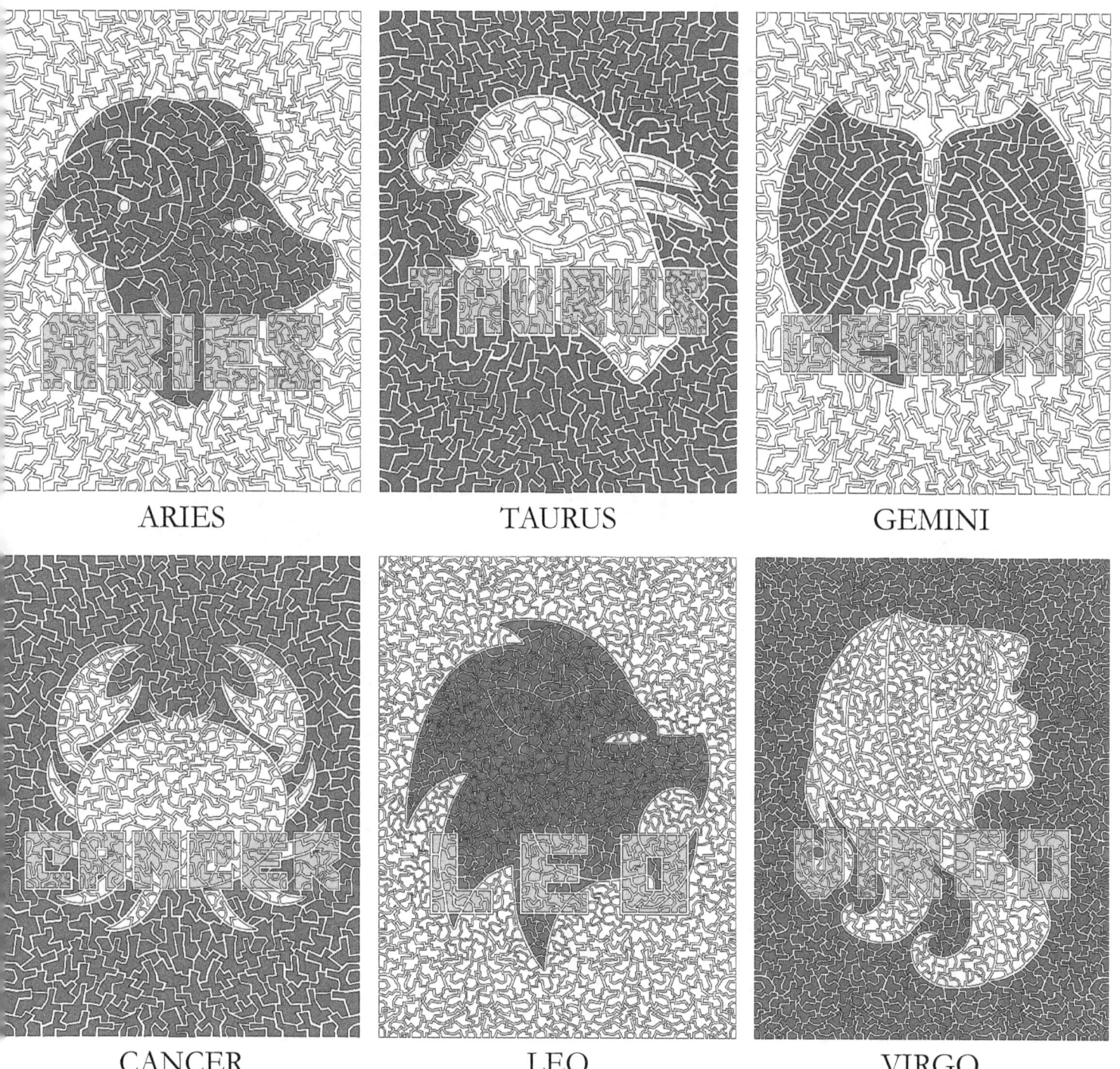

ARIES

TAURUS

GEMINI

CANCER

LEO

VIRGO

see more colored designs at **purplefishdigitalmedia.com**

COLORING GUIDES

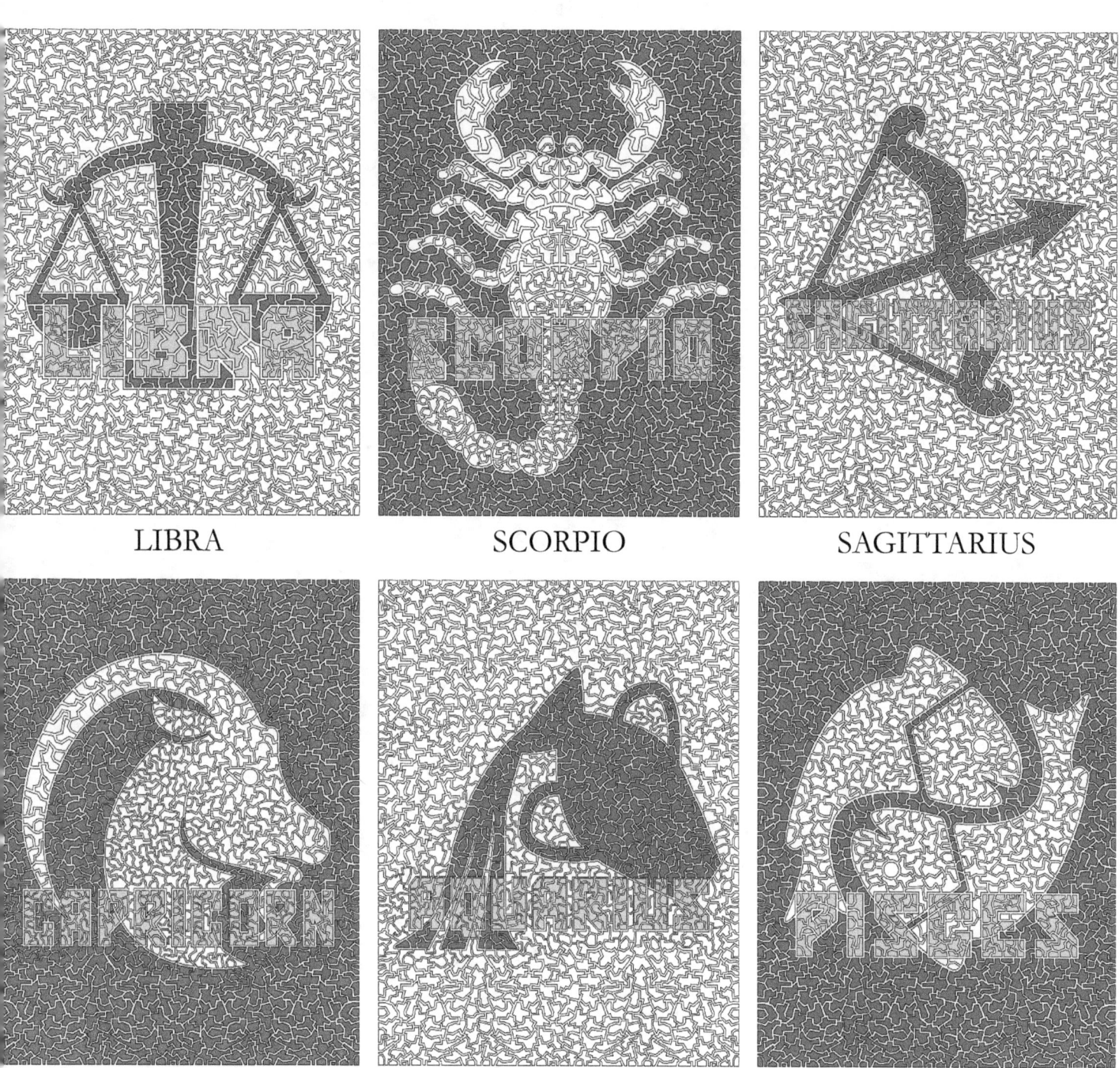

LIBRA

SCORPIO

SAGITTARIUS

CAPRICORN

AQUARIUS

VIRGO

see more colored designs at **purplefishdigitalmedia.com**

I Hope You've Had an Enjoyable and Imaginative Journey Coloring
The Big Zodiac Coloring Book!

please do visit **purplefishdigitalmedia.com** for more of my designs.